LAND TRANSPORT

Malcolm Dixon

**Illustrated by
Jones Sewell and Associates**

Exploring Technology

Houses and Homes
Communications
Flight
Land Transport
Machines
Structures
Textiles
Water Transport

For Joanne and Michelle

Series editor: Sue Hadden
Consultant: Mark Lambert
Designer: Malcolm Walker, Kudos Designs

First published in 1991 by
Wayland (Publishers) Ltd
61 Western Road, Hove
East Sussex BN3 1JD, England

© Copyright 1991 Wayland (Publishers) Ltd

British Library Cataloguing in Publication Data
Dixon, Malcolm, 1946–
  Land transport.
  1. Land Vehicles. Design
  I. Title II. Series
  629.04
ISBN 1–85210–966–1

Phototypeset by Nicola Taylor, Wayland
Printed in Italy by G. Canale & C.S.p.A.
Bound in France by A.G.M.

Cover: *A four-wheel-drive vehicle bounces across rough terrain in the Paris-Dakar Rally.*

Contents

On the move	4
The wheel	6
Making wheels	7
Bicycles and motorcycles	8
Looking at a chain drive	9
Cars, buses and trucks	10
Make a model car	11
Providing power	12
Using an electric motor	13
Make a powered vehicle	14
Gears	16
Making gears	17
Streamlining	18
Investigating streamlining	19
Supercars	20
Make a dragster	21
Road construction	22
Make a concrete road	23
Building railways	24
Locomotives	26
Make an electric locomotive	27
High-speed trains	28
Make a maglev train	29
Cable railways	30
An aerial cable car system	31
Amphibious vehicles	32
Make a hovercraft	33
Earth-moving vehicles	34
Make a bulldozer	35
Brakes	36
A hydraulic brake system	37
Safety	38
An automatic signal system	39
Space exploration	40
Make a planet-roving vehicle	41
The future	42
Build a wind-powered vehicle	43
Glossary	44
Further information	45
Index	47

On the move

In our modern world people are often on the move. We travel by road and rail to get to school or work, to visit friends, do the shopping and go on holiday. All over the world goods are transported by freight trains and trucks. There are millions of motor cars, trucks, buses, bicycles and trains travelling over a vast network of roads and railways.

The development of motorized forms of land transport – such as cars, buses and trains – has made it much easier to travel from place to place, and this has changed many people's lives. One hundred and fifty years ago most people worked very close to where they lived, and they could only buy products that had been made or grown locally. Today people are able to live a long distance from their place of work and commute each day. The goods that we buy in our local shops have often

We rely on many different forms of land transport in our everyday lives.

Computers are now very important in the design of vehicles. This engineer is using computer graphics to check the design of a new braking system.

been brought from a long way away. These changes have happened quite quickly, so quickly that they are sometimes called a revolution. This 'transport revolution' has not finished yet, because people are still finding faster and better ways of travelling on land.

Making road vehicles and trains that can move at high speeds, and yet be safe and comfortable to travel in, is a complicated job. The designers and engineers who do this job have many different things to consider, such as the best materials to use, the correct type of engine to provide the power and the ideal shape for the vehicle. They need to consult books and discuss their ideas with other people, and they must plan everything in advance. There are always many problems to be overcome before the vehicle they have designed is ready to be put to use.

This book explains how many different types of vehicles work, and gives you the opportunity to make models of them which will move on land. You will be able to build models from your own designs and to solve problems as they arise. There are chapters on how roads and railway systems are constructed, the importance of safety in the design of transport systems, and the ways in which methods of moving on land might change in the future.

The wheel

The wheel is one of the greatest inventions of all time. When early humans wished to move a heavy load they may have just dragged it. Later they discovered that rollers made the movement of a load easier. Rollers do not have to slide over the ground and so there is less friction. Logs of wood were placed under the load and as the load was pushed forwards so new rollers were placed in front of the load. This method was effective but slow.

It is believed that the wheel was first used in the Middle East, by the Sumerians, about 5,000 years ago. The first wheels were probably made from solid discs of wood. There is archaeological evidence that the Sumerians used three pieces of wood, clamped together using cross-struts, to construct their early wheels. Carts with four wheels and a pair of axles were later developed. Oxen were used to pull the carts. This type of wheeled transport spread to Europe and to China.

About 4,000 years ago a new type of wheel was produced. It consisted of an outer rim and a hub in the centre. The hub was joined to the rim by spokes, and two wheels were joined together by an axle. This design, which is light but strong, was very suitable for horse-drawn chariots and wagons.

Today wheels are everywhere and they are used in many different ways. Think of as many uses as you can for wheels. Collect pictures from newspapers and magazines to show the uses of wheels in land transport.

Wheels like those on this cart have been in use for around 4,000 years.

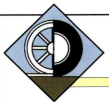

Making wheels

You need:
8 wooden ice lolly sticks (all the same size)
Cardboard
Pair of compasses
Scissors
PVA glue and a spreader
Hand-drill and 6-mm bit
Length of wood, 1 cm square
Flat piece of wood about 15 cm by 10 cm by 2 cm
Hammer and small nails
Hacksaw
Dowel rod, 6 mm in diameter
Plastic tubing of 6 mm internal diameter

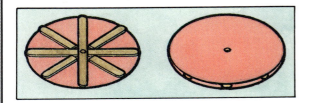

1. Measure the length of a lolly stick. Using the compasses draw two circles on a piece of cardboard; the diameter of the circles must be the same as the length of the lolly stick. Carefully cut out the circles. Glue one lolly stick to one cardboard circle, as shown. Ask an adult to drill a 6-mm hole through the centre.

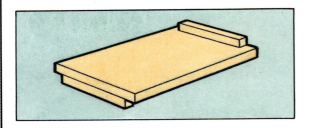

2. Next make yourself a bench-hook to help you cut the lengths of wood you will need. Nail or glue two strips of wood, each about 6 cm long by 1 cm square, on to the flat piece of wood.

3. Use the bench-hook and a hacksaw to cut three more lolly sticks in half and stick the six pieces on the card as shown. You will have to shorten them first so that they do not project beyond the card circle. Now glue the second card circle on top of the sticks. Leave your wheel to dry. Make a second wheel in the same way.

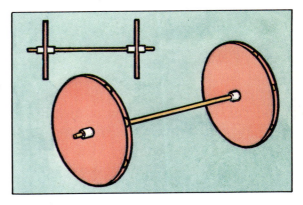

4. Cut four short pieces of the plastic tubing. Cut a piece of dowel rod about 15 cm long to make an axle. Slide a piece of plastic tubing on to each end of the axle, then fit the wheels, and finally slide on the other pieces of plastic.

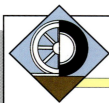
Bicycles and motorcycles

The bicycle is a human-powered form of transport which is popular all over the world. The machines that are in use today have evolved from bicycles built over the last two centuries. In 1791 a wooden machine was built in France. It was moved by the rider 'walking' the machine along. The first pedal-pushed bicycle was built in 1839 in Scotland by a blacksmith, Kirkpatrick Macmillan. His design used foot pedals, moving backwards and forwards, to drive connecting rods which turned the rear wheel. The 'penny-farthing' bicycle was invented in 1871. It had a very large front wheel and a smaller rear wheel. The front wheel was driven by the rider pedalling cranks fixed to the centre of the wheel.

Modern bicycles are driven by a

Modern racing bicycles are made from light, strong materials.

chain. A large sprocket, or chain wheel, is fitted on to the bicycle frame, and a smaller sprocket is fixed to the rear wheel. The two sprockets are connected by an endless chain. The rider turns pedal-cranks fitted to the larger sprocket. This moves the smaller sprocket and the rear wheel, and forces the machine to move.

The first motorcycle was built in France in 1869. A small steam engine was fitted to a bicycle with a pulley belt driving the rear wheel. Later designs used a petrol engine connected by a chain drive to the rear wheel. Motorcycles are now a fast and economical form of transport.

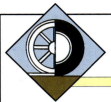

Looking at a chain drive

You need:
A bicycle

Look at the large sprocket on the bicycle. Notice how the pedals are fixed to it. Look carefully to see how the chain fits into the teeth of the large sprocket.

Ask a friend to lift the back wheel of the bicycle off the ground. Turn the pedals so that the large sprocket makes one complete turn. How many times does the back wheel turn? How far would the back wheel travel for one turn of the large sprocket?

Count the number of teeth on the large sprocket. How many teeth are there on the smaller sprocket? Can you see a link between these numbers and the number of times the back wheel revolves for one turn of the pedals?

Cars, buses and trucks

There are millions of cars on the world's roads. Their invention and production in huge numbers has revolutionized transport systems. Many people now have the freedom to travel by car wherever they want, provided a road or track is available.

Cars are built in a wide variety of shapes and sizes. Developing a new model from first designs through to mass production takes a great deal of work and is very expensive. Any new model of car includes thousands of different parts which must all work together to provide a safe form of transport. The designers have to decide what size and type of engine is best to use for the vehicle they are building. They must consider whether the engine should drive the front or the rear wheels and they will think about the brakes, the gearing, the steering, the suspension, the electrical system, the best materials to use and many other things. Prototypes will be built and tested. Finally, when the engineers are satisfied that the car is the best they can develop, then it will be made. Each day, thousands of new cars will be built on an assembly line using robots to fit the parts together.

Buses and trucks are just as important as cars in the world today. Modern buses can carry many passengers at great speed over long distances. Powerful trucks are used to move very heavy loads by road. Engineers are always working to make buses and trucks even better at their tasks.

Large trucks are used all over the world to transport goods by road.

Make a model car

You need:
Long, cardboard toothpaste box (or similar)
Rigid card
Bench-hook (see page 7)
4 wheels (see page 7)
Dowel rod, 6 mm in diameter
Hacksaw
Scissors, ruler and pencil
Plastic tubing of 6 mm internal diameter
6-mm hole punch
Brass paper fastener
PVA glue

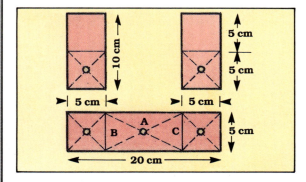

1. Cut out two pieces of rigid card each measuring 10 cm by 5 cm. Mark the cards as shown in the diagram and punch two holes where the diagonal lines cross.

2. Cut out another piece of rigid card 20 cm by 5 cm. Mark it as shown and punch 6-mm holes where the diagonals cross. Make a small hole at point A and press the paper fastener through. Fold the card along lines B and C.

3. Glue the two short pieces of card to the outside of the toothpaste box. Fix the large piece to the box with the paper fastener. It should be able to move freely.

4. Using the bench-hook and a hacksaw, cut two pieces of dowel rod, one 12 cm and one 15 cm long. Push them through the holes in the axle holders. Make sure the longest axle goes through the widest axle holder. The axles should turn easily.

5. Make four wheels (use the method on page 7) and fix them to the axles using small pieces of plastic tubing. Now test your car. Does it move easily when you push it, and does the steering work? How can you make your car look more attractive? Try using paint, cardboard and other materials.

 # Providing power

This is the engine of a powerful 'hot rod' car. It runs on petrol.

To power a vehicle an engineer needs a suitable engine. The earliest engines used steam, which was produced by burning coal. The steam moved a piston backwards and forwards inside a cylinder. This type of engine is called an external combustion engine because the source of heat is actually outside the engine. Most modern road vehicles now have internal combustion engines. A mixture of fuel (usually petrol) and air is sucked into a cylinder through an inlet valve as the piston inside the cylinder moves down. When the piston moves back up again it squashes the fuel and air mixture and a spark then sets the mixture alight. As the tightly packed mixture burns it expands and forces the piston downwards. The up-and-down motion of the piston moves a series of shafts and gears and eventually turns the wheels of the vehicle.

Some vehicles use a type of internal combustion engine called a diesel engine. The fuel it runs on is not petrol but diesel oil. The fuel mixture is ignited not by a spark but by the heat that is produced when air inside the cylinder is squashed very tightly by the piston.

The wankel engine is another type of internal combustion engine that was developed quite recently. The pistons inside a wankel engine do not move up and down inside their cylinders, but round and round. This is why wankel engines are sometimes called rotary engines. Some vehicles do not use combustion engines at all but are powered by electric motors and batteries.

Using an electric motor

You need:
Screwdriver and small screws
Small electric motor
4.5-volt battery
Wire
Crocodile clips
Flat piece of wood
Cotton reel
Elastic bands
Plastic tubing of 6 mm internal diameter
Hacksaw and scissors
Strong glue, e.g. Evostik (not superglue)
6-mm hole punch
Rigid card
Dowel rod, 6 mm in diameter
Paperclip switch

1. Use glue or screws to fix the electric motor to the piece of wood. Fix a small piece of plastic tubing to the end of the motor spindle. (You can use a blob of glue instead.)

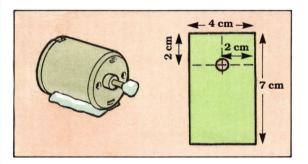

2. Cut two pieces of rigid card 7 cm by 4 cm, and punch holes in them as shown. Glue the pieces of card to the wooden baseboard.

3. Cut an axle from a piece of dowel rod long enough to fit through the holes in the cards. Before you fit it through the holes, push the cotton reel on to the axle and glue it in the centre. Pass an elastic band around the cotton reel; the band should be very loose. Push the axle through the holes in the cards and hold it in place with pieces of plastic tubing. Make sure the axle can spin freely.

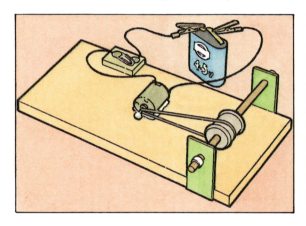

4. Attach the elastic band around the motor spindle. It should not be loose or too tight. If it doesn't fit properly you may have to try elastic bands of different lengths.

5. Attach wires, a paperclip switch and a battery to the motor as shown. Switch on and see how the motor turns the elastic band, the cotton reel and the axle. This type of electric motor-driven system is often used in road vehicles. You can use it to drive the model on pages 14 and 15.

Make a powered vehicle

You need:
Bench-hook (see page 7)
Some lengths of wood, 1 cm square
Small electric motor
4.5-volt battery
Wire
Paperclips
Hacksaw
Thin card
Rigid card
PVA glue
Ruler, scissors and pencil
6-mm hole punch
Dowel rod of 6 mm diameter
Cotton reel
4 wheels (see page 7)
Plastic tubing of 6 mm internal diameter
Insulation tape
Elastic band

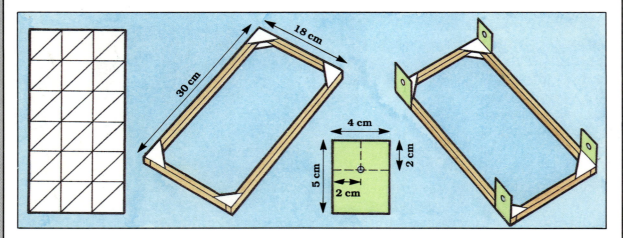

1. Use a pencil and ruler to draw horizontal, vertical and diagonal lines on a sheet of thin card. Cut out these card triangles as you need them.

2. Measure out two 16-cm lengths of 1-cm square wood. Place your bench-hook on the table and use the hacksaw to cut through the wood on top of the bench-hook. Ask an adult to watch while you do this. Cut two 30-cm lengths of 1-cm square wood using the same method.

3. Fix together the four pieces of wood you have cut to make a rectangular chassis. Make the corner joints by putting some PVA on card triangles and positioning them over the corners. Fix card triangles to both sides of each corner joint. Let the glue dry.

4. Cut four rectangles, each 4 cm by 5 cm, from the rigid card. Punch a 6-mm hole in each card. Glue one card to each corner of the wooden rectangle as shown. Let the glue dry.

5. Using the bench-hook and hacksaw, cut two 22-cm lengths of dowel rod. Slide a cotton reel on to one of these dowel rod axles and place an elastic band around the cotton reel. The band should hang loosely. Push the two axles through the holes in the cards. Make four wheels (see page 7) and fix them on the axles with plastic tubing. Make sure the axles turn freely.

6. Cut two 16-cm lengths of 1-cm square wood. Use glue and card triangles to fix them inside the rectangular wooden chassis, about 2 cm apart. Glue and tape a small electric motor to one of these lengths of wood. Put glue or a piece of plastic tubing on to the end of the motor spindle and attach the loose end of the elastic band. The band should not be loose or too tight.

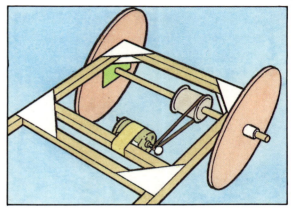

7. Tape a 4.5-volt battery across the two wooden struts inside the chassis, next to the motor. Connect the battery to the motor using wire and paperclips.

8. Switch on the motor. Does it turn the elastic band, the cotton reel, the axle and the wheels? Place your vehicle on the floor. Does it travel easily across the floor surface? Do you need to make any adjustments?

Design and make
9. Can you design and make a body shape for your vehicle? Use materials such as card, clear plastic, paper and kitchen foil and fix your shape to the wooden chassis.

Gears

A gear is a wheel with small raised projections, called cogs or teeth, around its edge. A group of gears all working together is called a gear train. The gears can be arranged so that their teeth interlock or 'mesh' together. When two gears of different sizes are meshed together, the smaller gear turns faster than the larger.

Gears can be made from a variety of materials, including cast iron, steel and plastic, and they are used in many different ways. In a car, for example, the engine provides the power which turns a crankshaft, and the movement of the crankshaft is passed to the road wheels through a group of gears called the transmission system. The gears reduce the speed of rotation but increase the turning power of the engine. A car driver uses the gears to control how much turning power the engine supplies to the wheels. Most cars have a gearbox containing four or five forward gears and one reverse gear. The driver changes from one gear to another using a gear lever attached to the gearbox. The gears are all of different sizes, and as the driver changes from a smaller gear to a larger one the amount of turning power supplied to the wheels increases and the car can go faster.

Most cars have a clutch that disconnects the engine from the gearbox while the gears are changed. Some cars have automatic gearboxes that change gear as the speed of the engine changes, so that the driver does not have to use the clutch and gear lever.

The cogs on these two gears are interlocking, or 'meshing' together.

Making gears

You need:
2 circular cardboard cheese box lids (or similar)
2 nails
Hammer
Scissors
8 wooden ice lolly sticks
Flat piece of wood, about 30 cm by 15 cm
PVA glue
Hacksaw
Bench-hook (see page 7)

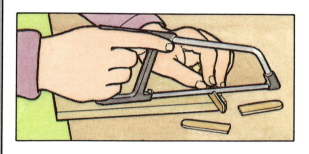

1. Cut the lolly sticks in half with the hacksaw on top of the bench-hook.

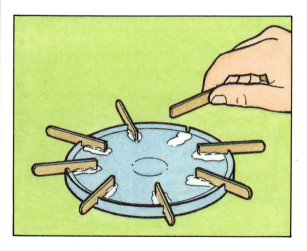

2. With scissors, cut eight slits at equal distances around the outer edge of each cardboard lid. Slide the half lolly sticks into the slits and glue them in place as shown. You now have two gears.

3. Make a hole in the centre of each gear and lay the gears on top of the flat piece of wood as shown. Make sure the teeth mesh. Fix the gears to the wood with the hammer and nails. Now turn one of the gears. What happens to the other one?

4. Try using this method to make gears of different sizes. Mesh them together to make gear trains.

Streamlining

Engineers spend a great deal of time and effort in ensuring that modern cars have streamlined shapes. A car with a streamlined shape can 'slice' through the air. This means it will be able to travel faster and use less fuel. Car designers say that these cars have a low wind-resistance or low drag factor. If a car is designed to travel very fast it is vitally important that its tyres stay in contact with the road, or the driver will lose control. So, in developing the shape of the car, the designers must make sure that as air passes over the car it presses downwards.

Many ideas for ordinary road vehicles have been tested first as racing cars. Look at the picture of a racing car. As air passes over the front spoiler and rear wing it presses down and helps the car to grip the road. When you look at many modern cars you will see that they often have front spoilers, sloping front bonnets and small rear wings. All of these design features allow the air to flow around the car and help with road-holding. Engineers often test the shapes of new car designs in a special wind tunnel to show that the air flows as smoothly as possible around them. Modern computer systems are now used in the design stages. They can calculate how air will flow around a car even before it has been built.

The spoiler and rear wing help to keep this racing car on the ground.

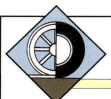

Investigating streamlining

You need:
Some wood, 1 cm square
Bench-hook (see page 7)
Hacksaw
Scissors
Thin card
Rigid card
6-mm hole punch
PVA glue
Wooden ice lolly sticks
Dowel rod, 6 mm in diameter
Plastic tubing of 6 mm internal diameter
Hairdryer

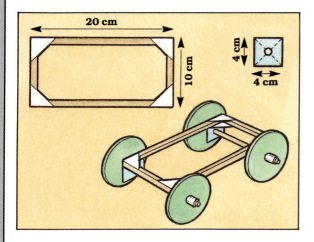

1. Using the method on page 14, make a chassis measuring 20 cm by 10 cm from the wood and triangles of thin card.

2. Use some rigid card to make four axle holders measuring 4 cm by 4 cm as shown and punch a 6-mm hole in the centre of each one. Glue the axle holders to the chassis as shown. Using the method on page 7, make four wheels of 8 cm diameter from card and lolly sticks. Cut two dowel rod axles 14 cm in length. Push the axles through the axle holders. Fix the wheels in position using small pieces of plastic tubing.

3. Design and make four different designs of car body shape which can fit over the top of your vehicle chassis. Use thin card and glue.

4. Plan an experiment to test the streamlining of the four car body shapes. Ask an adult to help you use a hairdryer to supply the 'wind' for your experiment.

Supercars

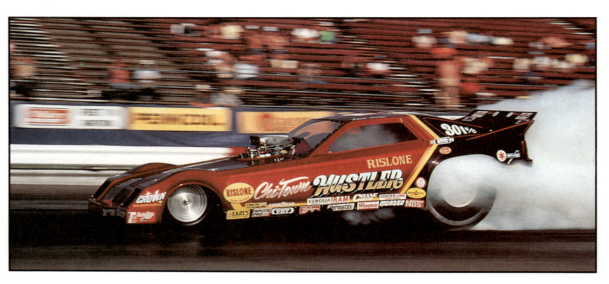

Dragsters are built to be light, strong, streamlined and very fast.

Grand Prix racing takes place on specially designed circuits in various parts of the world. The cars that take part must be built according to international rules which govern the engine size and other parts of the design. The cars are constructed using the most advanced techniques and materials. Because of the high speeds involved any poor material or design idea is soon detected. Some of the ideas used in racing cars have also been used to build 'supercars' to break the world land speed record. Malcolm Campbell, in 1935, travelled at over 480 km/h in his Bluebird car. More recently rocket-powered cars have travelled at 1,120 km/h.

Drag racing is a popular sport in the USA. A dragster is a special racing car which is designed to accelerate to a very high speed within a short distance. Some dragsters can move more than 400 m in less than six seconds. During this time they accelerate to over 320 km/h. They travel so fast that they often use a parachute to help them stop. The chassis of a dragster may be 7.5 m in length and be made of welded steel tubing. A strong but light design is required. Aluminium sheeting, which is also very light, covers the chassis and careful streamlining ensures that the dragster stays on the ground at very high speed. Powerful engines, with superchargers and fuel injection systems, are used to give rapid acceleration.

Make a dragster

You need:
Some wood, 1 cm square
Bench-hook (see page 7)
Hacksaw and scissors
Thin card
Rigid card
6-mm hole punch
Wooden ice lolly sticks
PVA glue
Dowel rod, 6 mm in diameter
Plastic tubing 6 mm internal diameter
Hand-drill with 6-mm bit
Elastic bands

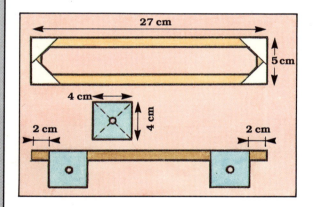

1. Using the bench-hook and hacksaw, cut two lengths of wood each measuring 25 cm, and another two each measuring 5 cm. Use the method shown on page 14 to make a chassis with the wood and some thin card triangles.

2. Cut four 4-cm square axle holders from rigid card. Punch a 6-mm hole in the centre of each, and then glue them to the chassis.

3. Use card and wooden lolly sticks to make two wheels of 5 cm diameter and two wheels of 9 cm diameter. (Use the method on page 7.)

4. Cut two 9-cm lengths of dowel rod and push them through the holes in the axle holders. They should turn easily. Using pieces of plastic tubing, fit the smaller diameter wheels to one axle. This will be the front of your dragster. Fit the larger wheels to the back axle.

5. Loop some elastic bands together and attach them, by another loop, to the front of the chassis. Twist the other end of the elastic around the back axle. Turn the axle round and round so that the elastic is stretched quite tight. Place your dragster on a table top or on a level floor and then let it go. Does it move fast?

Road construction

A road has to be carefully planned before building starts. The planners first need the answers to many questions. How many vehicles will use the road? Will heavy trucks use it? How fast will the vehicles travel? What sort of weather will the road have to stand up to? Can the materials needed to build the road be obtained near to the site of the road? What materials will be used for the top surface of the road? The route that the road will take needs to be mapped out and some buildings may need to be demolished.

The ground will be levelled by huge earth-moving vehicles (see page 34). Bridges and road tunnels may have to be built along the route of the road. To make the road foundations, layers of crushed stone and concrete will be used. To make it stronger the concrete may be reinforced with steel mesh. In some parts of the world, large blocks of polystyrene have been used to make the foundations. Finally, a top surface of asphalt or concrete will be laid.

Many modern roads allow vehicles to travel at high speeds over long distances. In Britain these roads are called motorways. In North America they are known as freeways or expressways. They are carefully designed to be fairly straight, with no sharp bends or junctions.

This new road bridge is made from concrete reinforced with steel.

Make a concrete road

You need:
Soil
Long cardboard box
Small trowel
Small stones or gravel
Sheets of polystyrene
Gloves
Large, empty tin can
Sand
Cement powder
Bowl to mix concrete in
Bucket of water
Scissors
Chicken wire
Flat piece of wood
Sheet of polythene

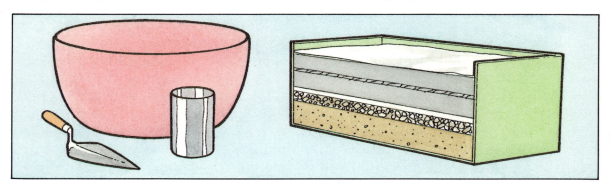

1. Put a layer of soil about 6 cm deep in the cardboard box and flatten it down with the trowel. Place a layer of small stones on top of the soil and then cover the stones with sheets of polystyrene. The soil, stones and polystyrene will form the foundations for your road.

2. Now make some concrete. First put your gloves on. Use the tin can as a measure, and measure out one can of cement powder, three cans of small stones and two cans of sand. Mix them all together in an old bowl. Stir in some water – not too much, as the mixture should be quite stiff. Use the trowel or a piece of wood to mix all the materials thoroughly.

3. With the trowel, spread the concrete mixture over the foundations until it is fairly flat. Then tap the surface with the trowel to push out any air bubbles. Cut out a piece of chicken wire and lay it on top of the concrete.

4. Make some more concrete as before, and spread it on top of the chicken wire. Tap the concrete again to push out the air bubbles. Smooth out the surface and make it level using a flat piece of wood. Cover the concrete with a sheet of polythene and leave it to harden.

5. Cut away one side of the box to show the layers of your road.

Building railways

When travelling by rail, passengers can move around the carriages, eat in a restaurant and, if they wish, sleep. They are comfortable and safe. They can travel from city centre to city centre at high speed without the worry of traffic jams. Freight trains carry goods long distances across the world. Today, railways are an important part of our lives.

Railways were developed in Britain over 190 years ago, and they soon spread to other countries, especially the USA. Railways are built over vast distances, through forests and across swamps and prairies. Tunnels are dug through mountains and under rivers, and bridges are constructed to carry railways across waterways, roads, gorges and other railway lines. Railway engineers try to keep the railway track as level as possible so that the train wheels do not slip on sloping tracks. Where the land begins to slope downwards an embankment is built. This is a bank of earth with a flat top on which the railway lines are laid. When hills have to be crossed the engineers dig through them to form cuttings.

Modern trains run along steel rails which are fastened to 'sleepers' made from heavy timber or concrete. These sleepers are laid on a foundation of broken stones, called ballast. Firm foundations are needed to support the huge weight of the trains on the rails. In hot weather the steel rails can expand.

Railway builders in the USA had to cross many natural obstacles.

A modern electric train crosses a bridge in a mountainous area of Japan.

This could cause them to buckle and force trains off the rails, resulting in serious accidents. To prevent this small gaps are left where two rails join. The two rails are held together by a pair of metal 'fishplates'. When you travel in a train you can often hear the clatter as the wheels pass over these gaps. Modern steel rails are welded together to form very long lengths. These rails are firmly fastened to heavy sleepers and fewer expansion gaps are needed. This makes train journeys much quieter.

The wheels of a train are made of steel and have a lip or flange on the inside edge. These flanges help trains to stay on the rails even when travelling around curves.

When you next travel on a train think of the problems the engineers may have had building the railway. Look out for embankments and cuttings. How many tunnels do you travel through? Do you travel under a river or through a mountain? How many bridges do you cross? Do you climb or descend any slopes? Look for passenger and freight trains. Listen to the sound of the wheels passing along the rails. Can you hear the regular clatter of the gaps in the rails or are you travelling on the modern larger rails? Find a safe position to look at some railway tracks. Are the sleepers made of wood or concrete? **Never go near railway lines**.

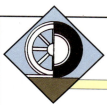

Locomotives

Trains are pulled by locomotives. These vehicles provide the power to pull or push the train carriages. For over a century all locomotives were powered by steam. Coal was burnt in a 'firebox' and it heated water in a boiler. Steam from the boiler moved pistons in cylinders and the movement was passed through rods to the driving wheels of the engine. George Stephenson and his son Robert built the famous Rocket locomotive in 1829. In 1938 a locomotive called the *Mallard* travelled at 202 km/h, while hauling seven coaches, and set the world speed record for steam trains.

In countries with no coal supplies of their own, it became cheaper to use electricity to power locomotives. In one method the electricity is supplied to the locomotives using overhead wires. The locomotives collect the electricity using a frame called a pantograph. Another method is to supply the electricity using a special rail called the conductor rail. The locomotive is fitted with metal 'shoes' to collect the power. Sometimes a fourth line is also used. The electricity drives electric motors which turn the wheels on the locomotives and enable them to move along the rails.

Many locomotives are driven by powerful diesel engines which run on a fuel called diesel oil. Usually the diesel engines operate an electric generator which supplies power to the electric motors that drive the wheels. This type of locomotive is called a diesel-electric. **Never go near electric railway lines or overhead cables**.

For many years, trains were pulled by steam locomotives like this one.

Make an electric locomotive

You need:
6 round coffee jar lids (screw-on)
Hand-drill and 6-mm bit
Some flat pieces of wood
PVA glue
Long, narrow cardboard box
Bench-hook (see page 7)
Hacksaw
Dowel rod, 6 mm in diameter
Plastic tubing of 6 mm internal diameter
Small electric motor
Plastic propeller
4.5-volt battery
Paperclips
Wire

1. Glue a small, flat piece of wood inside one of the coffee jar lids. Drill a 6-mm hole through the centre of the lid and the wood. Do the same to the remaining five lids.

2. Make six 6-mm holes near the bottom of the cardboard box as shown. Make sure that the holes along one side are in line with the holes along the other side. Cut three dowel rod axles to fit through the holes; they must be long enough to allow you to fit the wheels.

3. Fix the six wheels in place using pieces of plastic tubing.

4. Glue the motor to the top of the box as shown, and fit the propeller to the motor spindle. Leave the glue to dry. Connect the battery to the motor using paperclips and wire.

5. When you connect up the circuit the propeller should spin very fast and push your locomotive along a smooth floor or table-top.

6. Try to make your model look more realistic by gluing cardboard to the front. Paint your model to make it look more attractive.

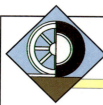

High-speed trains

The French TGV trains are some of the fastest in the world.

Railways have to compete with road and air travel for passengers. There is, therefore, a need to make trains that can go faster than ever before. In Japan electric-powered 'bullet' trains regularly run at 210 km/h between Tokyo and Osaka. The French have developed trains which can travel at 275 km/h. Many engineers believe that this speed is close to the limit for trains riding on rails. New developments for high-speed rail vehicles may do without wheels and use air-cushion lift (see page 32) or a system of magnetic levitation.

Trains using the magnetic levitation (or maglev) method have already been built and are operating in Japan. Powerful superconducting magnets, cooled by liquid helium, are used to lift and propel the train along the track. When fully developed these trains may be able to run at over 400 km/h. The ride will be smooth and almost silent because there will be no friction of wheels against the rails. Early maglev designs used a central guiding rail whereas newer plans suggest that the train will run between guiding walls.

Make a maglev train

You need:
Plasticine
2 strong bar magnets
Used matchsticks
Thin card
Scissors

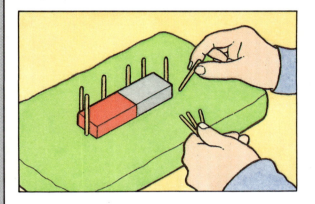

1. Roll out the plasticine to make a long, flat slab.

2. Place one bar magnet on the slab. Push some matchsticks into the plasticine around the edges of the magnet.

3. Take the second magnet and try to make it 'float' above the first magnet. Can you feel the force pushing them apart? Why do you need the 'wall' of matchsticks? Try the experiment without the matchsticks in place.

Design and make

4. Using thin card design and make a small train to fit on top of the floating magnet. Make the shape streamlined.

Cable railways

Cable railways are often used to transport passengers up steep slopes such as the sides of a mountain. The wheels of a conventional train would be unable to grip the track and would slide backwards. Usually a double track is built up and down the mountain. The cable cars, which are like small railway carriages, are linked together by cables. When one car is at the top of one track the other is at the bottom of the second track. An engine is used to pull the cable and move the cars up and down the track. This type of cable car system is called a funicular railway.

In some mountainous areas, such as Switzerland, another type of cable railway, with aerial cable cars, is used. Strong steel pylons are built on deep concrete foundations and steel cables are stretched between them. Large cable cars, sometimes carrying a hundred passengers, are suspended from these cables. Electric motors move the steel cables and so transport the cable cars up and down the mountain. Safety is very important because some pylons are spaced 1.6 km apart and the cables are over 300 m above ground level. Chair lifts, which carry single or twin seats, are another type of cable transport. They are often used by skiers.

Aerial cable cars can carry many people up and down mountains.

An aerial cable car system

You need:
Some lengths of wood, 1 cm square
Bench-hook (see page 7)
Hacksaw and scissors
PVA glue
Wooden ice lolly sticks
Thin card
Pair of compasses
Rigid, thick card
6-mm hole punch
Hand-drill and 6-mm bit
Dowel rod, 6 mm in diameter
Plastic tubing
String
Thin wire
Baseboard of wood or thick card

1. Build two pylons as shown out of wood and card triangles. Glue lolly sticks to the framework to provide extra strength. Glue a piece of rigid card, with a 6-mm hole punched in the centre, across the top of each pylon.

2. Make two pulley wheels out of circular pieces of card. For each wheel, glue thin card circles to both sides of a slightly smaller circle of thick card. Drill a 6-mm hole through the centre of each wheel.

3. Fix one pulley wheel to the top of each pylon using dowel rod and plastic tubing. Glue a small piece of dowel rod to the top of one pulley wheel to act as a turning handle.

4. Connect the two pylons together with strong string running around the pulley wheels. You may need to glue the ends of the string together.

5. Design and make some cable cars. Use paper or thin card so that they are light. Hang the cable cars from the string using thin wire.

6. Turn the dowel rod handle and make the cable cars move. Glue the pylons to a baseboard.

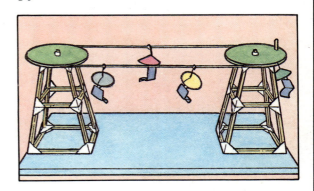

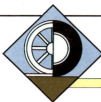

Amphibious vehicles

An amphibious vehicle emerging from the sea on to land.

Amphibious vehicles, sometimes called amphibians, can move both in water and on land under their own power. Many of these vehicles have been developed for military use. They are able to float in water and move using small propellers or water jets. On land, wheels or tracks are used for movement. All-terrain vehicles (ATVs) are popular in the USA and Canada as 'fun' vehicles providing road and water transport.

Air-cushion vehicles (ACVs), or hovercraft, are also able to move on land and on water. A hovercraft hovers just above the road or water surface supported by a cushion of air. A powerful hovercraft can travel much faster on water than a large liner, and far faster than most other amphibious vehicles. It has the great advantage of being able to move from sea to land easily. Once on land it can operate over snow, ice and rough ground. The air cushion is produced by propellers driven by powerful motors. It is kept under the hovercraft by a flexible 'skirt' which hangs around the edge of the vehicle. The hovercraft is pushed along by other propellers, and steered by rudders that deflect the airstream.

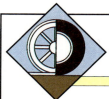

Make a hovercraft

You need:
Light plastic or polystyrene container
Marker pen
Small electric motor
Sticky tape
Scissors
Wire and wire stripper
Paperclips
Small plastic propeller
PVA glue
4.5-volt battery

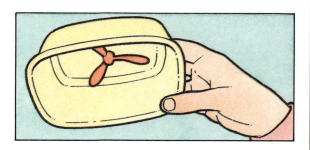

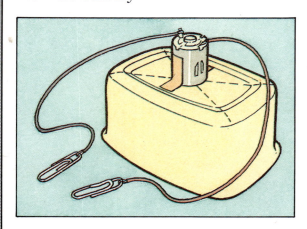

1. Mark diagonals on the bottom of the container as shown, and make a small hole where they cross.

2. Push the spindle of the electric motor through this hole and tape the motor in position. Cut two lengths of wire and remove the insulation from the ends using the wire stripper. Fasten one wire to each of the two motor connections. Attach a paperclip to the free end of each piece of wire.

3. Glue the propeller to the motor spindle. The propeller should turn without touching the sides of the container.

4. Place your hovercraft on the floor and attach the paperclips to the battery. Does your hovercraft lift off the floor?

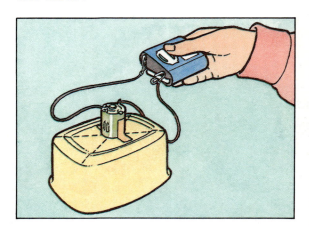

Design and make

5. Design and make a skirt to go around the edge of your hovercraft. What materials would be best to use? How can you fix the skirt to the hovercraft? Does the skirt make your hovercraft lift further off the floor?

Earth-moving vehicles

When engineers are building roads and railways, they have to move millions of tonnes of earth from the site. Special vehicles have been built to help them. Scraper and grader machines are often used. The scraper is a vehicle with a knife-like cutting blade that can slice off layers of soil and rock. The depth of the layer of earth to be scraped off can be varied by adjusting the cutting blade. The earth that is removed is forced into a large container inside the vehicle and then transported to a dumping site. Large diesel engines provide these vehicles with tremendous power. Huge wheels and tyres help them to move around on rough terrain. When most of the earth has been removed from the site, grading vehicles set to work. A grader also has a cutting blade. It produces a more precise, flatter finish to the surface.

Bulldozers are used all over the world to move earth and make land flat. Crawler tracks allow bulldozers to move easily over very rough ground. Like scrapers, bulldozers are powered by diesel engines. There is a large blade at the front of the vehicle to shift loads.

This bulldozer is pushing a large load of soil with its blade.

Make a bulldozer

You need:
Cardboard boxes
Thin card
PVA glue
Bench-hook (see page 7)
Hacksaw
Dowel rod, 6 mm in diameter
Foam pipe insulation
4 cotton reels
Plastic tubing of 6 mm internal diameter
Corrugated cardboard
Thick card
4 paper fasteners

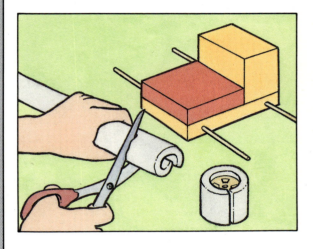

1. Glue together some cardboard boxes and thin card to make a bulldozer shape.

2. Make four holes near the base of the bulldozer. Using the bench-hook and hacksaw, cut two dowel rods to act as axles. Push them through the holes and make sure that they turn easily.

3. Cut some pipe insulation into four sections and fit each one around a cotton reel. Push the cotton reels on to the axles and fix them in place with pieces of plastic tubing.

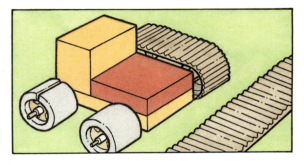

4. Cut two lengths of corrugated cardboard to make crawler tracks. Fit one track around each pair of wheels and glue the ends together.

5. Use thick card to make the front blade of the bulldozer. Fix it to the bulldozer body with paper fasteners and thick card. Push your bulldozer along. Does it move easily?

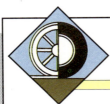

Brakes

The brake discs on this racing car are so hot they are glowing red.

You have discovered some of the ways in which vehicles can be made to move. But how do they stop? Many vehicles are fitted with brakes called 'drum' brakes. Curved brake 'shoes' are pushed against the inside of a rotating drum. The shoes are pushed by compressed air or by hydraulic fluid – liquid which is under pressure. When the brake shoes and the drum rub together the friction slows down the rotation of the drum. Disc brakes are now used on many modern cars. A foot pedal is connected to the brakes by thin tubes containing hydraulic fluid. When the pedal is pressed down it pushes against the hydraulic fluid which forces two brake shoes on to the sides of a revolving disc, causing the disc to slow down. The materials used for the shoes, drums and discs of brakes need to provide a great deal of friction, and be hard-wearing.

Like cars, lorries and buses, railway trains also use drum and disc brakes. They are usually operated by compressed air. The air is passed down the entire length of the train through a pipe, and so long as the air is compressed the brakes stay off. When the air pressure is reduced all of the brakes on the train are applied at the same time. Have you ever noticed the communication cord or alarm handle in a train? In an emergency, if the cord or handle is pulled, air is released from the compressed air pipe and the brakes are applied automatically.

A hydraulic brake system

You need:
2 flat pieces of wood
Hammer and nails
Empty tin can
2 plastic syringes
Plastic tubing
Water
Sticky tape

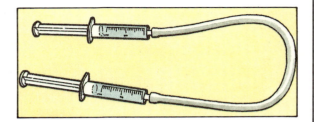

3. Join the syringes together with plastic tubing. Fill the tube and syringes with water – this is best done underwater in a sink or bath, to prevent air bubbles getting in. Press the plunger of one syringe. What happens to the other syringe?

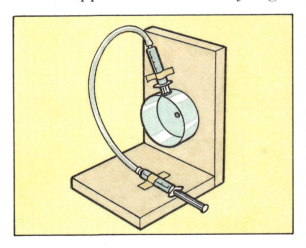

1. Fix the pieces of wood together to form an L-shape using the hammer and nails.

2. Find the centre of the base of the tin can and hammer a nail through it. Fix it to the wooden upright as shown. Spin the tin can and make sure it revolves easily around the nail.

4. Fix one syringe to the wooden upright using sticky tape. Then tape the other syringe to the baseboard. Spin the tin can and then press the syringe on the baseboard (imagine it is the brake pedal of a car). The plunger of the second syringe (the car brake) should be pushed against the tin can (the car wheel), forcing it to slow down.

Safety

As land transport has developed, road vehicles and trains have been made faster and faster. What is more, there are now more vehicles on the roads than ever before. Because of these factors, accidents happen every day. Engineers try to think of ways to reduce the number of accidents. Dual-circuit brakes and anti-lock braking systems, for example, have made some cars safer to drive.

Cars are designed to try to protect the driver and passengers if an accident occurs. Special safety glass is used in the windows. Some cars have rigid cages and body sections that crumple on impact, leaving the section in which people sit relatively undamaged. Seat belts also protect people in accidents, and collapsible steering wheels, padded head-rests and padded interiors all help to reduce injuries.

Cat's-eyes in the road reflect light from car headlamps to tell drivers which side of the road they are on. Crash barriers are used on motorways and some other fast roads to prevent vehicles crashing into oncoming traffic. They are usually strong enough to stop vehicles breaking through them. Traffic lights, sometimes controlled by computers, can reduce the number of accidents at road junctions.

Signalling systems are also used on railways. They tell train drivers when to stop and when it is safe to go. Many railway accidents have been caused by human mistakes. Automatic safety devices and computers are increasingly being used to reduce the chances of human error and so prevent accidents.

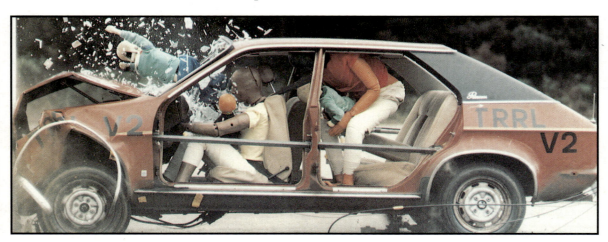

A simulated accident. The dummies without seat belts are thrown forward.

An automatic signal system

You need:
Thin card
Scissors
Kitchen foil
Glue
Wire
Wire stripper
4.5-volt battery
Bulb holder and 3.5-volt bulb

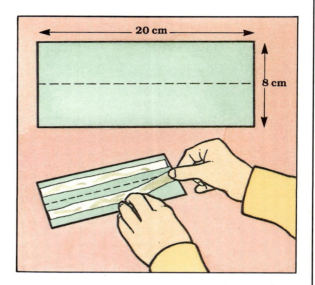

1. Cut a piece of card measuring 20 cm by 8 cm. Cut two pieces of kitchen foil 20 cm by 2 cm. Glue the foil strips to the card as shown.

2. Remove the insulation from the ends of two lengths of wire using the wire stripper. Push the wire-ends between the foil and the card as shown. Make sure they are firmly fixed and that the wires are touching the foil. Carefully fold the card along the dotted line. You have made an automatic switch.

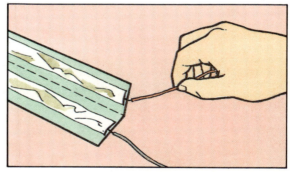

3. Connect the other ends of the wires to the battery and bulb holder, and join the battery and bulb holder together with another piece of wire. Place your automatic switch on the floor or on the road you made (page 23). If you drive one of your vehicles over the switch does the light go on? Does it go out again when the vehicle has passed? Try using a buzzer instead of the bulb. Can you work out how this automatic signal system works?

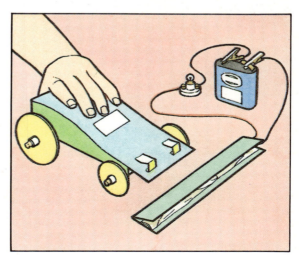

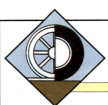

Space exploration

People have already begun the exciting challenge of exploring space. Rockets and spacecraft have been developed and men have landed on the moon. In 1970 the USSR built and placed on the moon the first lunar vehicle, called Lunokhod 1. This robot vehicle was controlled by radio signals from earth. A large panel of solar cells made electricity from sunlight. The electricity was used to drive Lunokhod's eight wheels and control the television cameras and other scientific instruments that were carried on the vehicle.

The USA has also landed a vehicle on the moon. The Apollo 15 astronauts, Scott and Irwin, used a Lunar Roving Vehicle to explore the moon's surface. It was electric powered and had a maximum speed of 16 km/h. The wheels were made of wire mesh. Both astronauts were able to sit on the vehicle and could travel about 65 km if they wished. A television camera and aerial sent pictures back to earth. When the astronauts returned home they left the vehicle on the moon.

This is the Lunar Roving Vehicle that was taken to the moon as part of the Apollo 15 mission.

Make a planet-roving vehicle

The problem:
Design and build a model planet-roving vehicle. It must be able to carry two passengers and move over a planet's surface.

Materials to use:
Empty washing-up liquid bottles
Pieces of wood, 1 cm square
Plastic tubing of 6 mm internal diameter
Bench-hook (see page 7)
Hacksaw
PVA glue
Dowel rod, 6 mm in diameter
Elastic bands
Electric motor
4.5-volt battery
Paperclips and wire
Wooden ice lolly sticks
Thin card
Thick, rigid card

The method:

1. Collect ideas – look through this book and at other books in libraries to find some ideas. Think how you might power your vehicle: with an electric motor or a stretched elastic band, perhaps. Will you use small or large wheels? What will you use to make the wheels? How big will you make the chassis?

2. Make drawings – as ideas come to mind, make sketches.

3. Select your best idea – think carefully about all of your ideas and decide which one you think will work best. Make an accurate drawing of the one you choose.

4. Construct your model – build the vehicle you have designed. First test it on a smooth surface and then try it on a rough surface. Have you solved the problem? How could you modify your model to make it work even better?

The future

Manufacturers are continually developing road vehicles that give better performance while using less fuel. In many advanced car engines the fuel is injected into the cylinder. This gives more power than if the fuel is simply sucked in by the movement of the pistons. Special alloys, which are lightweight but strong, are used to make sure the engines run at maximum efficiency. Some cars are fitted with turbochargers which use the normally wasted exhaust gases to boost the power of the engine. To reduce air pollution, a device called a catalytic converter can be fitted to the exhaust system of a car. These trends to improve performance, to reduce fuel costs and air pollution, to use new materials and to fit increasingly advanced computer systems, will almost certainly continue. Some people predict that in the future road vehicles will not need drivers because computers will be able to drive safely and find the correct route from place to place.

Petrol engines may be phased out altogether and be replaced by ones that use a more 'environmentally-friendly' fuel, or by electric engines. Cars are now being developed which use electric engines for short-distance driving and a normal combustion engine for motorway journeys. Public transport may well be improved with better and faster railway and bus systems. The bicycle will continue to grow in popularity as a cheap and healthy form of transport. As in the past, changes in land transport methods will probably transform our lives.

Do you think cars of the future will look like this?

Build a wind-powered vehicle

You need:
Pieces of wood, 1 cm square
Bench-hook (see page 7)
Hacksaw
PVA glue
Scissors
Thin card
Rigid card
6-mm hole punch
6 cotton reels
Dowel rod, 6 mm in diameter
Foam pipe insulation
Plastic tubing of 6 mm internal diameter
Sheet of polythene

1. Build a chassis 25 cm by 35 cm using wood and thin card triangles (see page 14). Glue a sheet of rigid cardboard to the top of the chassis. Glue two cotton reels to the cardboard as shown.

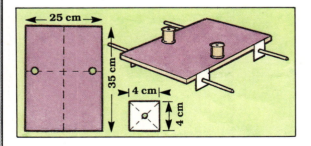

2. Cut four axle holders measuring 4 cm square out of rigid card and punch a hole in the centre of each. Glue the axle holders to the chassis. Cut two 34-cm lengths of dowel rod and push them through the axle holders. Do they turn easily?

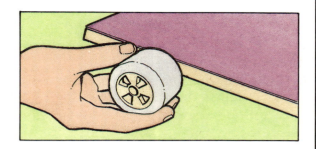

3. Make four wheels using cotton reels and pipe insulation (see page 35). Fit the wheels on to the axles and hold them in place with plastic tubing.

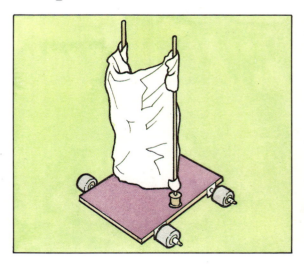

4. Cut two 50-cm lengths of dowel rod to make masts. Push them into the cotton reels on top of the model. Glue them firmly in place. Cut a square of polythene and stick it to the masts to make a sail. Test your model outside on a smooth area of concrete. How far does it travel? Do you need to make any modifications?

43

Glossary

Alloy A mixture of two or more metals.
Anti-lock brakes A braking system designed to prevent skidding when the brakes are applied suddenly.
Assembly line A system in which workers or robots are each responsible for one job in the making of, for example, a car.
Axle The shaft to which the wheels of a vehicle are attached.
Brake A device used to slow down or stop a vehicle.
Catalytic converter A device fitted to a vehicle's exhaust system to reduce the amount of pollutants in the exhaust gases.
Chassis The framework on which a vehicle is built.
Clutch A device to disconnect a vehicle's engine from the gearbox.
Commute To travel some distance regularly, such as between home and school.
Cylinder The tube inside which a piston moves in an engine.
Dual-circuit brakes (dual braking system) A braking system with two circuits, so that if one circuit fails the other continues to operate.
Engine A device that converts one sort of energy into another.
Exhaust system The means by which exhaust gases are removed from an engine.
Friction A force that tends to prevent sliding between surfaces in contact.
Fuel A substance that produces energy in the form of heat.
Fuel injection system A way of pushing fuel into the cylinders of an engine.
Internal combustion engine An engine in which the fuel is burnt in a cylinder and drives a piston.
Maglev Magnetic levitation.
Mass production Making identical objects in very large numbers.
Piston A part that moves up and down in the cylinder of an engine.
Prototype The first vehicle built to a new design.
Spoiler A device designed to use the pressure of moving air to hold a car firmly on the ground.
Supercharger A device, driven by the engine itself, that forces air into the engine and boosts performance.
Superconducting magnet A magnet made with superconductors so that a strong magnetic field can be maintained without continually using electric power
Superconductor Something through which an electric current can pass without any of the energy being lost.
Vehicle Any machine that can transport people or goods.

Further information

Books to read

Clark, D. *The Car* (Marshall Cavendish, 1978)
Dixon, M. *Young Engineer on the Railway* (Wayland, 1983)
Dixon, M. *Young Engineer on the Road* (Wayland, 1983)
Jollands, D. (Ed.) *Machines, Power and Transport* (Cambridge University Press, 1984)
Jones, J. *Powered Vehicles* (Blackwell, 1987)
Kurth, M. *Engines* (World's Work, 1973)
Lambert, M. *Car Technology* (Wayland, 1989)
Pepper, W. *Car Factory* (Franklin Watts, 1984)
Pick, C. *Railways and Trains* (Macdonald Educational, 1978)
Roberts, D. *The Invention of Bicycles and Motorcycles* (Usborne, 1978)
Tuck, R. *Mountain Movers* (Patrick Stephens, 1984)

Organizations to contact

Education Service
Science Museum
Exhibition Road
London SW7 2DD

British Rail Education Service
Euston House
P O Box 100
24 Eversholt Street
London NW1 1DZ

Bus and Coach Council
Sardinia House
52 Lincoln's Inn Fields
London WC2A 3LZ

Ford Motor Co Ltd
Public Affairs
Eagle Way
Brentwood

RoSPA
Cannon House
The Priory Queensway
Birmingham B4 6BS

Remember to send a stamped, addressed envelope with your enquiry.

Places to visit

National Railway Museum
Leeman Road
York

Science Museum
Exhibition Road
South Kensington
London

Greater Manchester Museum of
Science and Industry
Liverpool Road
Manchester

The Tank Museum
Bovington Camp
Wareham
Dorset

National Motor Museum
Beaulieu
Hampshire

Great Western Railway Museum
Farrington Road
Swindon
Wiltshire

Yorkshire Dales Railway Museum
Nr. Skipton
Yorkshire

Beamish Open-Air Museum
Chester-le-Street
Tyne and Wear
Nr. Durham

London Transport Museum
Covent Garden
London

Ffestiniog Railway Museum
Harbour Station
Porthmadog
Gwynedd

Midland Motor Museum
Stourbridge Road
Bridgnorth
Shropshire

Grampian Transport
Museum and Railway Museum
Alford
Aberdeenshire

National Curriculum

This book will be useful to teachers in implementing the National Curriculum at Key Stages 2 and 3. The information and activities relate to:

Technology attainment targets 1 ,2, 3, and 4

Science attainment targets 1 ,5, 6, 10, 11 and 13

Land Transport could also be developed as a cross-curricular topic that includes National Curriculum English and Mathematics.

Index

Accidents 38
Air-cushion vehicles 32
All-terrain vehicles 32
Amphibious vehicles 32
Anti-lock braking 38
Apollo 15 40
Automatic gearbox 16

Bicycles 4, 8–9, 42
Brakes 10, 36, 38
Bridges 22, 25
Britain 22, 24
Bulldozers 34–5
Bullet trains 28
Buses 4, 10, 36

Cable railways 30–31
Campbell, Malcolm 20
Canada 32
Cars 4, 10, 16, 18, 20, 36, 38, 42
Carts 6
Catalytic converter 42
Cat's-eyes 38
Chair lifts 30
Chassis 20
China 6
Clutch 16
Coal 12, 26
Communication cord 36
Conductor rail 26
Crankshaft 16
Crash barriers 38
Crawler tracks 34
Cylinders 12, 42

Designers 5, 10, 18
Diesel engines 12, 26, 34
Diesel-electric locomotives 26

Diesel oil 26
Drag factor 18
Dragsters 20–21
Dual-circuit brakes 38

Earth-moving vehicles 22, 34–5
Electric motors 12–13, 14–15, 26–7, 30, 42
Engineers 5, 10, 12, 18, 24, 25, 38
Engines 5, 8, 10, 12, 20, 26, 42
Expressways 22
External combustion engine 12

Fishplates 25
France 8, 28
Freeways 22
Friction 6, 28, 36
Fuel 12, 18, 42
Fuel injection 20
Funicular railways 30

Gearbox 16
Gears 10, 16–17

Hovercraft 32–3

Internal combustion engine 12

Japan 25, 28

Land speed record 20
Locomotives 26
Lunar vehicles 40
Lunokhod 1 40

Macmillan, Kirkpatrick 8
Magnetic levitation 28–9

47

Mallard 26
Mass production 10
Materials 5, 16, 20, 22, 36, 42
Moon 40
Motorcycles 8
Motorways 22, 38

Oxen 6

Pantograph 26
Penny-farthing 8
Petrol engines 12, 42
Pistons 12, 42
Pollution 42
Prototypes 10

Racing cars 18, 20
Rails 24–5, 26, 28
Railway building 24–5
Railways 4, 5, 24–5, 38
Road construction 22–3
Roads 4, 5, 22
Robots 10
Rocket 26
Rocket-powered cars 20
Rollers 6

Safety 30, 38
Seat belts 38
Signalling systems 38

Sleepers 24, 25
Solar cells 40
Spoiler 18
Steam engines 12, 26
Steering 10
Stephenson, George and Robert 26
Streamlining 18–19, 20
Sumerians 6
Supercharger 20
Superconducting magnets 28
Suspension 10

TGV trains 28
Tour de France 8
Traffic lights 38
Trains 4, 5, 24–5, 26, 28, 36
Transmission system 16
Trucks 4, 10, 36
Tunnels 22, 25
Turbocharger 42
Tyres 18, 34

USA 20, 24, 32, 40
USSR 40

Wankel engine 12
Wheels 6–7, 12, 16, 34, 40
Wind resistance 18
Wind tunnel 18

Picture acknowledgements

The photographs in this book were supplied by: Allsport *front cover*, 8, 18, 20, 36; Eye Ubiquitous 12, 25, 26, 32; Mansell Collection 24; Quadrant 42; Topham 5, 6, 16, 28 (Associated Press); Transport and Road Research Laboratory 38; ZEFA 4, 10, 22, 30, 34, 40.
All illustrations are by Jones Sewell and Associates.